ALEX
WOOLF

Badger Publishing Limited
Oldmeadow Road,
Hardwick Industrial Estate,
King's Lynn PE30 4JJ
Telephone: 01438 791037

www.badgerlearning.co.uk

2 4 6 8 10 9 7 5 3

The Mayans ISBN 978-1-78464-067-5

Text: © Alex Woolf 2015
Complete work © Badger Publishing Limited 2015

Publisher: Susan Ross
Project editor: Paul Rockett
Designer: Jo Digby Designs

Picture credits:
© Aflo Co. Ltd./Alamy 14; akg-images 26; © Tibor Bognár/CORBIS 30; Reconstruction of a Mayan painting from Chichen Itza (Yucatan, Mexico) depicting a battle scene. Mayan Civilization./De Agostini Picture Library/G. Dagli Orti/Bridgeman Images 28; © D Alderman/Alamy 7; The Art Archive 23; © The Art Archive/Alamy 9, 22; © heather bean/Alamy 13; Priest in ceremonial robes, Isle of Jaina (clay & paint), Mayan/Private Collection/Photo © Boltin Picture Library/Bridgeman Images 8; ByronAguilar/Shutterstock 15; © Independent Picture Service/Alamy 17; © incamerastock/Alamy 16; akg-images/François Guénet 18; akg-images/Mel Longhurst 10; Man in a sacrificial position against a step, Classic period, 250-950 AD (stone), Mayan/Museo Nacional de Arqueologia y Etnologia, Guatemala City/Bridgeman Images 21; © Enrique Perez Huerta/Demotix/Corbis 12; Michael Rahel/Shutterstock 25; © ROYER Philippe/SAGAPHOTO.COM/Alamy 20; Yummyphotos/Shutterstock 4, 24; soft_light/Shutterstock 29; CC. Wikimedia Commons cover, 6, 11, 19.

Attempts to contact all copyright holders have been made.
If any omitted would care to contact Badger Learning, we will be happy to make appropriate arrangements

THE MAYANS

Contents

Vocabulary

Do you know these words? Look them up in a dictionary and then see how they are used in the book.

archaeologists

civilisation

compound

descendants

embroidered

epidemic

hieroglyphics

mythology

1. WHO WERE THE MAYANS?

The Mayans were a people who lived in Central America. They first appeared in the Yucatan Peninsula in about 2400 BCE. They built cities there, and developed astronomy, calendars and writing.

By 900 CE, the cities were mostly deserted. The Mayan civilisation had come to an end. However, the descendants of the Mayans continue to live in Central America today.

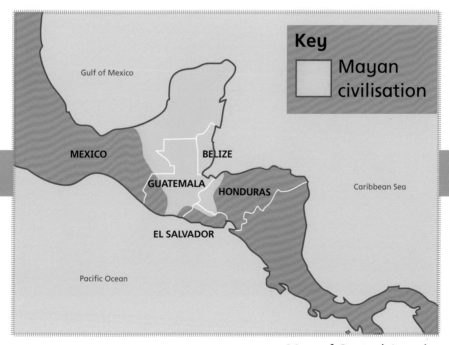

Map of Central America

2. THE MAYAN PEOPLE

For most of their history, the Mayans lived in small villages as simple farmers.

From around 250 CE, they began clearing areas of rainforest and building large cities connected by well-constructed roads. Every city had a central plaza, temples and a ball court.

El Castillo, a large temple pyramid in the Mayan city of Chichen Itza in Mexico

The Mayans were a highly skilled people. They made fine pottery, jewellery and richly decorated clothing. They charted the movement of the planets, developed a number system and wrote books about medicine, history and nature.

Decorated Mayan pot, from Honduras, made some time between 700 and 900 CE

HISTORY HIGHLIGHT!

The Mayans did not have metal tools. They built their cities using tools of stone, wood and shell.

Mayan rulers

The Mayans did not have a single ruler. Each city was controlled by a noble family who made the laws. They were advised by a team of officials.

The priests were also very powerful. They interpreted the will of the gods, and told people things like when to plant crops, who to marry and when to go to war.

Mayan priest figurine dressed in ceremonial robes, from the Isle of Jaina in Mexico

Class system

Mayan society was organised into classes.
The nobles and priests were at the top. Below
them were the craftsmen, traders and warriors.
At the bottom were farmers and then slaves.

People didn't often move out of their class.
Sons of warriors became warriors. Sons of farmers
became farmers.

Illustration of Mayan farmers at work

Households

Mayans lived in thatched huts. Extended families often lived in a compound of several huts built around a courtyard.

Compounds also included workshops, steam baths and tombs and shrines of ancestors. Most families would cook and eat together in the courtyard.

This is a reconstruction of a Mayan house from Chichen Itza. The walls are covered in adobe (sun-dried clay).

Children and school

Most children did not go to school. From the age of five they helped their parents in their work. Boys learned from their fathers, girls from their mothers. By the age of fifteen they were seen as adults.

The children of nobles were taught by priests. They learned about mathematics, science, astronomy, medicine and other subjects.

Scene of learning painted onto a ceramic pot

Food

The most important food of the Mayans was corn. They made tortillas from corn flour.
They also grew sweet potatoes, beans, chillies and squash, and hunted wild turkey, deer and ducks. Women tended vegetable plots and cooked and served meals.

This carving shows a Mayan god next to a cocoa tree. Cocoa beans were incredibly valuable. They were used as money as well as for drinking chocolate.

Clothing

The Mayans made clothes from cotton and hemp, woven into colourful designs. Women wore loose tops and long skirts tied with a colourful belt or sash. In winter they wore thick shawls. Men wore loincloths, skirts and ponchos.

For festivals, people dressed in richly embroidered clothing decorated with feathers and pompoms. They wore elaborate hats and jewellery.

The colourful clothes worn by the Mayans influence designs that are sold today.

3. CITIES

All Mayan cities were built in the same way. They had a large central plaza surrounded by temples, pyramids, a palace and a ball court. The plaza was used as a market and a gathering place for ceremonies and festivals.

Famous Mayan cities include Tikal, Palenque and Chichen Itza.

Remains of the ancient Mayan city of Palenque in Mexico

Pyramids

The Mayans built pyramids as tombs for members of the ruling family. The pyramids were also used for religious ceremonies. Some had steps leading to a temple at the top; others were not meant to be climbed.

HISTORY HIGHLIGHT!

The tallest pyramids were up to 60 metres high and could be used as landmarks in the rainforest.

The top of this pyramid temple in Tikal stands out above the treetops.

Palaces

Mayan palaces were large buildings, usually with several stories, where the ruling family would live. They were generally made of stone.

Some were very large with several courtyards and towers. Community feasts and dances may have been held there.

Remains of the large palace in Palenque

Ball courts

The Mayans played a ball game for fun, but also to honour their gods. The courts had a hoop at one end. The aim was to put a rubber ball through the hoop. Players could only touch the ball with their hips, feet and arms.

Sometimes prisoners of war were forced to play. They always lost. After the game, they were sacrificed.

A hoop on the wall of the ball court in Chichen Itza

4. GODS AND DEMONS

The Mayans believed in many different gods.
The most important god was Itzamna, god of fire.
He created the Earth and ruled heaven, as well as
night and day.

Other powerful
gods were
Kukulcan, the
snake god, and
Bolon Tzacab,
god of storms.

Statue of the god
Itzamna

18

Afterlife

The Mayans believed that after people died they had to travel through a dark underworld called the Place of Awe. Here the dead souls were tormented by demons before they finally reached heaven, the home of the gods.

The Mayans believed their ancestors watched over them from heaven.

This pot shows a chaotic scene of life in the underworld.

Demons

People feared that if they did not worship in the right way, the demons from the Place of Awe might come into the world and attack them. Priests wore fierce masks at ceremonies to scare the demons.

HISTORY HIGHLIGHT!

Mirrors were seen as very dangerous. The Mayans thought that if you looked into a mirror, the demons could suck you into the Place of Awe.

Modern-day re-enactor wearing the ceremonial dress of a high priest

Sacrifice

To keep their gods happy and ensure good harvests, the Mayans sacrificed animals and humans. Human victims were often prisoners of war.

The victim was laid on top of a pyramid or platform and the priest would cut open his chest and rip out his heart.

This stone carving shows a man leaning back in a sacrificial position – waiting to have his heart cut out.

4. ART AND SCIENCE

The Mayans were highly skilled artists. They carved pictures of their gods in stone, wood and jade. Many Mayan carvings have been found on large stone slabs called stelas.

They also painted murals on the walls of their buildings. These depicted scenes from daily life, mythology, battles and ceremonies.

Image of a warrior returning from battle with a severed head, carved into a wall in Chichen Itza

Ceramics

The Mayans made pottery without the use of a potter's wheel. They decorated their pottery with colourful designs and scenes.

They also made small clay statues. In tombs of nobles, archaeologists have found statues of ball players, servants, dwarfs, musicians and priests. They may have been put there to serve their lords after death.

Clay figure of a Mayan chief with headdress

Writing

The Mayans invented their own writing system. The system used both pictures and symbols, known as hieroglyphics. There are about 800 symbols. Archaeologists have worked out what most of them mean.

Mayan writing has been found on stelas, pottery and also in books made of soft bark that fold up like a fan.

This series of glyphs are from Palenque. They recorded details of events and the people who lived there.

Astronomy

The Mayans were keen astronomers. They believed the will of the gods could be understood by studying the sky. They worked out the cycles of the Sun, Moon, stars and planets and could predict events such as solar eclipses.

Temples and pyramids were built so that the Sun or Venus would be visible through certain windows at important times of year.

Observatory in Chichen Itza

25

Calendars

The Mayans used their knowledge of astronomy to create calendars. They had a religious calendar called the Tzolk'in, made up of 260 days.

Another calendar, the Haab', was used by ordinary people. It consisted of 365 days divided into 18 months of 20 days each and one short five-day month.

These pages are from the Madrid Codex, a book that recorded religious and domestic events that took place on each of the 260 days of the Tzolk'in calendar.

Mathematics

To work out astronomical cycles and create calendars, the Mayans needed mathematics. Their number system was based on 20 (not 10, like ours). This was probably because they counted on both their fingers and toes.

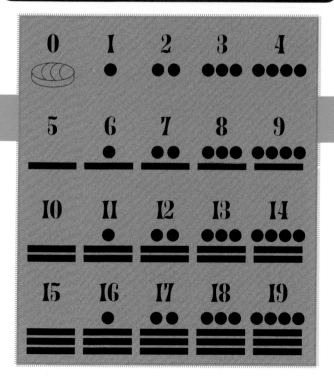

HISTORY HIGHLIGHT!

Unusually for ancient peoples, the Mayans included zero in their number system.

5. THE END OF THE MAYANS

Mayan civilisation came to an abrupt end during the late ninth century CE. No one knows why, but experts believe there were probably a number of causes:

1. Natural disaster: an earthquake, volcano or epidemic disease may have destroyed cities and killed tens of thousands of people.

2. War: Mayan cities often fought each other. This may have weakened them.

Reconstruction of a battle painting, from Chichen Itza

3. Famine: as populations grew, it put pressure on farmers to provide more food. A few bad harvests could have caused mass starvation.

4. Climate change: sea levels may have risen around the time of the Mayan collapse. This would have forced coastal people inland, putting strain on cities.

The Mayans today

The Mayan people did not disappear. Their lands were taken over by Spanish conquerors in the sixteenth century, but Mayan culture survives to this day.

Their heritage is preserved in their colourful traditional clothing, the languages they speak and in their stories and legends.

QUESTIONS

When did the Mayans start building their cities? *(page 6)*

Why were the priests powerful? *(page 8)*

At what age did a Mayan become an adult? *(page 11)*

What was the Mayans' most important crop? *(page 12)*

In the ball game, with which parts of the body could you touch the ball? *(page 17)*

How did priests try to scare away the demons during ceremonies? *(page 20)*

Why did the Mayans study astronomy? *(page 25)*

Name one reason why Mayan civilisation might have collapsed. *(pages 28-9)*

INDEX